The Seven Laws of Productivity

The Seven Laws of Productivity

Make Your Vision a Reality

Emmanuel Goshen

Published by Edson Consultancy

© Copyright Edson Consultancy 2015

THE SEVEN LAWS OF PRODUCTIVITY

ISBN 978-0-993-06615-3

Printed and bound in the United Kingdom

Contents

Contents

I would like to dedicate the success of this book to

the Almighty God,

the foundation and pillar of wisdom.

I would like to dedicate this page to my family and friends all over the world, most especially my mother, whom made me understand that responsibility has no other meaning other than, "being up and equal to challenges in one's life. Pastor, Mrs. Victoria Majekodunmi, Master Edward Majekodunmi, Prophet Larry Osoffo, Prophet Moses Olurin, Mr. and Mrs. Kuku would all be remembered in my prayers for their various forms of support which made my vision of writing this book a reality.

PREFACE

Nothing reflects an organization's worth or ability more than productivity. In a nutshell, leadership and productivity are closely linked, because they are dependent on each other. Productivity is synonymous with getting things done with few resources. As we know, to achieve anything in life, reasonable action needs to be taken to get things done, but if anyone is merely completing tasks, it will inevitably amount to nothing. The first step to be taken by anyone aiming to be productive is to have a clear vision, which needs to be communicated clearly to ensure the commitment, will, and motivation of others to achieve an objective within a reasonable time frame is capable of becoming a reality and not a mere dream.

Generally speaking, the higher the productivity of an organization, the more stable it becomes in light of change of external factors. It could afford to change strategy provided the required resources are available to keep the organization moving. However, productivity takes time, requiring deliberate choices, patience, and perseverance. The fact remains that every small step taken enhances an increase in the level of productivity and makes an organization experience growth. If those steps are sustained and consistent, it could have a big impact on both the income and the stability of an organization. Productivity is ultimately the product of individual and organizational decisions about how to generate value.

To sustain an organization, there has to be an improvement at all levels of an organization because it increases the capability of an organization to maintain a better position within an industry. However, according to Dr John Maxwell, in his book The 15 Invaluable Laws of Growth, the first law, the law of intentionality, states that growth doesn't just happen, it's one step after another. In tough economic times, the major challenge facing most organizations is the ability to survive and sustain a better position within the marketplace and to also seek improvement measures to keep the organization afloat. This is the major activity that reflects an organization and its leaders as being productive.

INTRODUCTION

A law is a statement that requires compliance, regardless and irrespective of those that pass it or make it come to reality. It could be regarded as a platform that promotes the common good of all; after all, it was made for the purpose of checks and balances. It must be followed. Those who don't follow the law will face certain consequences or penalties. However, in order to fully understand a law, it's necessary to understand the ongoing situation that called for it to be recommended, passed, enacted, and enforced.

The Laws of Productivity must be complied with for any leader or manager to be productive in both the workplace and in everyday occurrences. Being productive is the only way to avoid failure. The story of the men in The Leaders Supplement, another of my books, reflects the beauty and advantages of being productive and also keeps managers in line for better opportunities.

In general, laws are made to ensure the rights of citizens against abuses by other people, by organizations, and by the government itself. Laws are made to provide for the general safety of all citizens in any given state. The law serves as a guide towards getting things done in a correct and acceptable manner. Likewise, the laws of productivity serve as a framework for leaders to be and remain productive. I remember the importance of the Road Traffic Act, which serves as a guide for appropriate parking and traffic flow in the United Kingdom. The law applies to every motorist, regardless of gender, age, or class, largely in the areas of obeying traffic signals or speed limits. Parking restriction is another important aspect of the traffic act that facilitates various parking policies across the country. It is up to the motorist to know and understand the rules in any area before parking; without this understanding, one might be fined for what he or she thinks to be right but is actually in violation of the law. Ignorance of the law is inexcusable. The traffic rules must be complied with to keep all motorists safe.

Productivity is about the effective and efficient use of all resources. A life or a leader without a vision or a goal would rarely be productive. To have deep insight into productivity, one needs to know the required resources, which include time, people, knowledge, information, finance, equipment, space, energy, and materials, in terms of their strategic impact in meeting organizational needs.

Productivity is an essential element in understanding what exactly needs to be done to meet stakeholders' needs. Leaders are required to establish a proper plan for execution and define their implementation strategies to complete all activities and tasks efficiently. A leader who doesn't understand what it means and takes to be productive is similar to a boat on the ocean without a sailor to steer it—it has no direction or destination. Without doubt, the boat would be lost in a matter of time. Such is the case with organizations without effective and productive leadership. Productivity requires a leader to stand for something, in addition to taking the appropriate action at the right time to arrive to the best solution and achieve the best possible outcome. Leaders must constantly monitor bottlenecks and obstacles, identify variances, and take the relevant actions to correct them or modify plans to make their results worthwhile.

The real responsibility for productivity or performance improvement should be largely in the hands of leaders rather than the individual workers. When leaders rely too much on team members to get things done, they typically lose the respect of the entire team. For leaders to be productive, they need to learn how to set their priorities so as to enable them to focus on what's important. They must have a realistic schedule to control, be able to handle various situations, and strive to avoid wasting time—the ingredients of productivity. From experience, most great people are able to achieve great things, simply because they were acutely aware of how to manage their time, energy, and financial resources while having perfect insight into and knowledge of the way to get where they want to be.

However, people who procrastinate get easily distracted by incorrect information, believing if only the world was flat they would've done just fine. In a nutshell, they don't get a lot done; instead, they give up too soon. As a matter of fact, procrastination is the major reason some leaders are not as productive. Procrastination kills their ability to deliver expected results for organizational stakeholders.

The fact remains that the fewer excuses a leader makes, the more chances he or she has to succeed—productivity is not just about knowing how to get things done; it's about accomplishment. One of the parables tells the story of the need for effective stewardship, that is, leaders are rewarded for every effort they make towards meeting the expectation of stakeholders. The story also reflects that after every project, leaders are held to account.

DRIVERS OF PRODUCTIVITY

Organizational stakeholders don't consider previous performance or achievement – only the most current results matter. Organizational leaders and CEOs are faced with ever-increasing expectations and must keep an organization going regardless of its internal and external resources. According to Newton's Second Law of Motion, acceleration occurs when a force acts on a mass. The greater the mass (of the object being accelerated) the greater the amount of force needed (to accelerate the object). However, for leaders to be productive and gain an edge over rivals, they require extra knowledge and skills to drive an organization towards greater achievements. They must get the best out of all resources invested in an organization and must also constantly monitor rival activities in the marketplace to determine when it's the best time to change existing plans to remain competitive.

In both theory and practice, productivity is the relationship between an expected output and the invested input required to make it a reality. However, the difference between organizational input and output reflects how productive and reliable leaders and their team are and their potential status in terms of meeting future challenges. Productivity as a whole reflects the quality, profitability, and efficiency an organization relies on for the purpose of maintaining a better position within an industry. However, the ability of leaders to aim towards a good level of productivity serves as a driving force to make the best use of every resource an organization possesses, including human resources, capital resources, monetary resources, and raw materials. Knowing the roles of each resource is not enough; the leader must recognize the impact of each resource.

Most managers and leaders see human resources as the process of recruiting, selecting, training, and developing staff; industrial relations; social investment; and the health and welfare of employees. However, it goes beyond those: A strong platform is required for focusing on sourcing and engaging the right people with the right skills at the right time in a way that's not only smart but incredibly cost effective in meeting both the current and the future needs of an organization. For productivity to be realistic, an organization needs to develop the right personal and professional capabilities of individuals and teams to help achieve and support its strategic objectives and meet future challenges.

The Law of Productivity is a matter of identifying and applying realistic measures in attaining a high level of effectiveness and efficiency both within an organization and in everyday situations.

In a nutshell, effective productivity is not about how resources are being used. Rather, it's about their impact in ensuring that organizational targets are being met. This proves and reflects the quality of leadership and management within the organization at all levels. For an organization to be productive, its leaders need to ensure that organizational processes are smooth and capable of meeting the needs of the customer at various points, and these things reflect the fitness and effectiveness of any leader.

I advise clients in coaching seasons that the beauty of every operational process is productivity, which enhances the expected utility to all relevant stakeholders and should be effectively supported to get the best in terms of quality. Leaders need to concentrate on developing and maintaining an effective information system for development activities such as learning and training in order to guarantee the best employee performance. Organizational leaders also need to research possible measures for staff to access and acquire transferable skills for their personal and career development purposes. However, due to huge stakeholder expectation and competition in the industry as a whole, organizations need to expand their use of modern learning technologies where appropriate and cost effectively enable accessible and remote learning solutions for all staff, irrespective of their working hours or location to keep productivity at the peak.

Being productive as a leader requires the ability to facilitate a wide range of operational needs and to design a suitable strategic direction for an organization. Productivity involves the ability to:

- Determine the specific requirements for operational needs
- Identify and understand stakeholders' responsibilities and expectations
- Identify and obtain support from operational experts

Furthermore, the above-mentioned operational needs have made a huge impact in ensuring productivity takes place within an organization. Here's a look at each component.

DETERMINE THE SPECIFIC REQUIREMENTS FOR OPERATIONAL NEEDS

It is paramount for leaders to understand the need for employees to be independent thinkers by giving them the chance to make decisions and use their discretion rather than stick to written policies, which might not be the best course of action when it comes to handling certain new situations or approaches to a problem. This situation creates a reasonable platform for developing untapped and undiscovered talents in various individuals and also making them responsible in decision-making. However, organizations need to ensure that team members have the right knowledge, skills, and abilities to perform up to expectations without any doubt or fear. In most cases, leaders need to look for certain competencies in team members to determine the quality and standard of their skill so they know what is expected of them at various points. These competencies include adaptability, analytical skills, action orientation, communication, customer care/focus, accurate decision-making, interpersonal skills, operational/planning skills, teamwork, and problem-solving abilities. An individual can never possess all the required skills for a team to be outstanding, but when each member plays his or her special role in line with their strengths, it become very easy to reflect the impact and importance of team dynamics, which in turn facilitates effectiveness.

To summarize, when determining the specifics for operational needs, leaders need to identify relevant capabilities that are significant for the implementation of process towards achieving the overall objectives of an organization. In leadership as a whole, achieving aims and objectives is usually done through the joint application of experience in terms of handling operational and organizational activities within various business areas of an organization. In addition, one's knowledge of related processes could also be required in facing down challenges, especially in terms of shortages and unexpected situations. Another reason leaders need to determine the specific requirements for operational needs is for the purpose of designing and delivering effective learning solutions for individuals and teams at all stages of their development, with the aim of making them productive. This should include providing professional support in the form of coaching and mentoring, which enables an organization to create more room for improvement. Profitability is the reason for productivity, which requires that all efforts be coordinated and integrated to reflect quality improvement. Leaders are expected to know the actual requirements for quality improvement, which enables them to forecast and plan for perfect implementation strategies aimed at retaining customers and avoiding the waste of resources. These strategies reflect long-term success in organizational activities.

It is widely acknowledged that an improvement in productivity is the key to the future economic growth and well-being of any organization. The main factor affecting productivity is the impact of change in government policy, which determines the way leaders design their platform for operational conduct to remain within the legal and regulatory frameworks. The reason for change in government policy most times is in the interest of the public as a whole. Leadership in terms of productivity is about commitment and dedication to increasing an organization's productivity level, focusing on capacity-building within an organization to enhance efficiency and effectiveness in its overall activities. These are essential parameters in solving both performance and implementation problems. They are also operational requirements that leaders need to identify and understand, else it becomes easier to be displaced by competitors within the same industry.

Through my contributions to various projects in leadership, strategic and operational management research, articles, and journals, I came to realize that for an organization to attain a high level of productivity, that is, the quality that differentiates them from others within an industry with the aim of edging out their competition, there must be a continuous improvement process that facilitates attaining and maintaining a better strategic position within the marketplace. Leaders need to learn from mistakes because "the best leaders are the best learners," and "because without mistakes it can never be possible to highlight where improvement is required. However, when any leader thinks about the ability to practice and learn—that is, such a leader is ready to give what it requires to improve—then mistakes aren't really mistakes. Rather, there are major steps towards identifying and understanding **THE 7 LAWS OF PRODUCTIVITY.**

IDENTIFY AND UNDERSTAND STAKEHOLDERS' NEEDS AND EXPECTATIONS

Attaining a leadership position and understanding the respective needs and expectations of relevant organizational stakeholders are two different things. Understanding this fact would enable leaders to focus more on major key areas in the interest of continuous improvement. However, stakeholders have either influence or interest in the performance of an organization. Having the right strategic insight regarding possible occurrences would enable leaders to set the right stage for expectations in relationship to their roles or responsibilities. The first key in understanding stakeholders, regardless of the organization's size, is the ability of leaders to clearly identify the different stakeholder groups and understand their level of influence both within and outside the organization. Leaders should take stakeholders' opinions, priorities, and concerns into account when planning and making decisions, developing and reviewing strategies, and supporting policies.

It is also important for leaders to consider how an organization will establish and maintain dialogue with different stakeholder groups to make use of effective processes and approaches in aligning and prioritizing stakeholders' various needs and wants in order to avoid conflicts, setbacks, and breakdowns in operational processes that would damage the reputation of an organization. Large-scale consumers and trade unions are two strong stakeholders that leaders need to watch; their actions can send many messages to the outside world. Large-scale consumers could easily change the game in the marketplace by making competing products more available to retailers and end-users as a result of an increase in discounts from competitors or new entrants to the market. Trade unions can affect the forecasted budget by demanding more than expected in the interests of employees, which could lead to conflict or strike, affecting outputs in a negative way in the long run.

In terms of understanding the needs and expectations of stakeholders, we must also understand their responsibilities, goals, and relationships with management of an organization, including:

- Providing the required resources such as time, money, and skills to enhance the smooth running of an organization's operational activities
- Giving a specific direction and making timely decisions to make strategic planning a reality
- Setting priorities, costs, and a review process in case of inflation
- Communicating and adjusting information that indicates the latest changes or developments promptly for others to see and understand the big picture

In a nutshell, the rights and responsibilities of stakeholders effectively define the conflict of interest between management and the various stakeholders within an organization. Leaders need to be open and honest in terms of dialoguing in the interest of all parties and the future of the organization as a whole. Leaders also need to embrace effectiveness and set realistic measures when making decisions regarding expected performance and quality improvements. Another way to increase engagement within an organization is to escalate stakeholders' involvement in the decision-making process, to give a sense of belonging and to gain more commitment and support for the purpose of productivity. As it's commonly said, "No involvement, no commitment" in which is as good as no achievement.

A good leader can also increase engagement through the way he interacts with his or her team. If leaders keep their distance and manage through a command-and-control style, or make decisions via a helicopter view, stakeholders will have a negative view of that leader, who facilitates no commitment. When, on the other hand, stakeholders feel as though they have a part in the decisions, they will feel more involved in organizational activities. It shifts their thinking and makes them more committed.

IDENTIFYING AND OBTAINING SUPPORT FROM OPERATIONAL EXPERTS

Leaders never get it done alone; there is always the need to get the support of others, especially experts. The desire for productivity as a whole requires leaders to remain focused on encouraging and developing a dynamic and highly-skilled workforce that can enable an organization to meet the expectations of organizational stakeholders and withstand the waves of competition. A team of experts plays several roles, among them, to help seek out and equip major organizational components in creating, building, and maintaining a safe and healthy financial status; to meet future challenges such as researching and developing new products; to keep up with the changes in customers' taste and fashion; to carry out mergers and acquisitions; and to obtain credit from financial institutions for the purpose of expansion. Surrounding oneself with a team of experts enables one to attain a good level of productivity while utilizing few resources because they help draw a strategic and realistic platform for reducing energy consumption, minimize waste generation, and give value for money for stakeholders' investment. However, leaders should learn to reason with others, especially during complex situations that require tough decision-making.

It becomes easier to think and act strategically when a leader has a pool of insight and ideas flowing and originating from various individuals with different backgrounds and experiences. Experts help draw a convincing route in achieving organizational goals by linking up strategic plans and giving each component individual measurable goals. However, the components serve as the drivers of productivity.

Having examined the major drivers of productivity in various situations, we can look at how those drivers are applied. The application of the drivers emphasizes the need for leaders to align everyone within an organization, regardless of their stakes, towards better performance. Those drivers are also major parameters for leaders to understand the importance of building and promoting effective leadership and management capabilities within an organization, creating productive workplace cultures and values, encouraging innovation and the use of technology, investing in people and skills, and networking and collaborating within and outside an organization.

PRODUCTIVITY WITHIN AN ORGANISATION

According to Robertson Cooper, the need to increase the performance and productivity of the workforce is very frequently cited as the number-one priority. However, traditional approaches like competency-based performance management, working smarter and implementing the commonly known LEAN strategies have typically already been 'done' in business. In reality, the search for new drivers of performance or, in the private sector, new sources of competitive advantage, is never-ending. Productivity is a matter of applying relevant and realistic steps towards success, and the fact remains that any leaders without the desire for productivity are far away from attaining success. The good thing about leaders and their teams being productive is that it enables an organization as a whole to tap into a new source of competitive advantage/performance improvement. It enables leaders to set realistic and achievable performance goals and measures. However, it also enhances the capability of individuals and teams to develop and improve skills and knowledge to create a culture of wellbeing. Productivity in leadership as a whole enables organizations to balance challenges with support by using pressure positively to drive performance.

For an organization to be productive, it is up to the leaders to first establish structure, responsibilities, and accountabilities, which reflect what an organization's leadership stands for. A productive leader would always consider it a major responsibility to plan, coordinate, control, mobilize employees, and monitor productivity programmes for the benefit of an organization. They are happy to introduce productivity measurement and performance management systems and also execute productivity improvement initiatives and ensure that they are continuously being implemented.

In a nutshell, productivity within an organization is leaders having the continuous ability to develop and clarify the organizational mission, policies, and objectives; establish formal and informal organizational structures as a means of delegating authority and sharing responsibilities; set priorities; and review and revise objectives in terms of change in demands from various stakeholders. In addition, the leader must maintain effective communications within various working groups and within the organization as a whole. Finally, a leader must select, motivate, train, and appraise staff; secure funds and manage budgets; and evaluate accomplishments and make various officeholders accountable for their actions. These are all parameters that make both leaders and organizations productive.

There are various aspects within an organization that leaders need to work on to establish productivity. Let's take a look at each one in the following section.

MANAGEMENT AND LEADERSHIP

When talking about management and leadership in terms of achieving goals to remain productive, both managers and leaders specify who is in control, responsible, and accountable for specific decisions and actions, alongside the impact on the organization as a whole. Many thanks to Mr. Loveday Cole, my former manager during my public service days, who made me, understand the need for sensitivity as a manager or a leader because one would be made accountable for the action of others. Employing the service of operational experts would allow a manager or leader to design a better operational platform for others to execute while setting their expectations and limitations. Many say that both leadership and management are all about control and taking responsibility, but applying an in-depth understanding, it goes beyond that—leadership is setting a new direction or vision for an organization to be in line with as a whole, while management controls or directs all forms of resources in accordance with achieving a specific goal within a specific time frame. Both management and leadership within most organizations play a huge role in creating and establishing the value that differentiates them from competitors. Both managers and leaders have it in their hands to empower and motivate others to attain effectiveness and efficiency. Leading and managing others is not all about power or organizational policies. Rather, it's about implementing the right action or policy in the right pattern at the right time.

The impact of both leadership and management within an organization remains inevitable due to its importance in strengthening an organizational reputation, improving employees' morale, having the ability to attract the best employees, and being able to discover and win new business to improve productivity and increase operational efficiencies. Leadership is the ability of an individual to influence, motivate, and enable others to contribute toward the effectiveness and success of the organization (House, 1996).

However, they both involve the ability to influence people to take actions towards completing a goal. In project management, for example, projects contain a number of components—the main three being scope, cost, and time. For the project team to effectively meet the goals of scope, cost, and time, one must appreciate the impact of positive leadership because it ensures that things are done in the right manner and at the right time. It is up to the project manager to manage issues related to scope, cost, and time, as well as to lead the team to successful completion of these goals and the project as a whole.

Management and leadership as a whole have been identified as a strategic area of importance in most organizations in both the private and public sectors. According to research, individuals holding management and leadership positions found it easier to influence people and situations both within and outside an organization for the purpose of achieving results and facilitating innovation and change.

The support of experts enables leaders to have a keener insight on how best to bring together different stakeholder perspectives to build a shared understanding of an organization's wider operational systems and processes, organizational strengths, and the underlying issues and dilemmas an organization faces. This process would enable the creation of a shared vision for productivity that supports the core purpose of an organization.

Regardless of the size of an organization, challenges remain inevitable in implementing the appropriate mix of change interventions at different levels of an organization. However, leaders need to focus on external factors such as political, cultural, and industrial dimensions in terms of impact and relevance, so as to remain capable in facing down challenges and remaining productive. In meeting with and facing down challenges, leaders need to learn the structures and systems that need to be integrated into a model that can be adapted to an organization in a way that is suitable for continuous assessment. Surveys can also facilitate leaders' understanding of their present management style and abilities in relationship to the challenges they face both internally and externally. However, taking insights from current results or feedback can help highlight grey areas for improvement and further developments.

Another strong challenge being faced by most leaders is in forming their teams. However, the ability to clearly define the structure of a particular team under a predetermined team formation model is an essential requirement because it facilitates the creation of a realistic vision, an acceptable pattern of behavior, and an understanding of the teamwork and operation model, which reflects high-performance leadership. A little faith and belief in oneself goes a long way in pulling a mountain of challenges down, regardless of the fear they create. Overcoming the fear being created by challenges is what I personally consider as taking a positive or good risk, which depends on one's mindset. In a nutshell, having a positive mindset enables leaders to build a set of skills that includes relationship-building, problem-solving, and effective listening, which are serious and applicable tools in facing challenges, especially during tough times.

INNOVATION AND TECHNOLOGY

Taking insights from Apple Incorporated, which was founded by the late Steve Jobs, Steve Wozniak, and Ronald Wayne, the first model of the Apple product was known as Apple I, which was assembled with a homemade wooden case. Now, the company produces MacBook Air, which is an ultra-thin, ultra-portable notebook. It was introduced in 2008 as a result of continuous advancement and innovation. Embracing innovation is one of the best ways to edge out competitors. Introducing a new item to the market is not typically a radical change, but rather a series of marginal utilities, that is, introducing features that give consumers value for their money and differentiate the product from other similar products. Innovation generally refers to changing or creating more effective processes, products, and ideas and can increase the likelihood of a business succeeding. Creativity is about having and making new ideas relevant to an organization's operational processes or activities to enhance effectiveness, which needs to stand and pass the test of able implementation. However, the outcome of creativity is innovation. The function of the internet, for example, is an example of innovation, because e-mailing, file-sharing, instant messaging, and other functions were not as easy and convenient years ago. I remember the use of paper files, which needed to be passed around tables and offices by some junior employees, with no guaranteed security or confidentiality. The introductions of instant messaging helped organizations reduce the cost of postage. Promoting an innovative culture is a better way of increasing organizations' capacity, that is, human resources, which includes the number of employees and their quality, skills, and experience; physical and material resources such as machines, land, and buildings; financial resources like money and credit facilities; information resources, which deal with the pool of company knowledge and databases; and intellectual resources, which cover an organization's copyrights, designs, and patents.

Innovation and motivation are inextricably linked to the generation and reduction of uncertainty, albeit in very different ways.

Leaders need to embrace innovation and new technologies to survive and thrive in a dynamic world, to enable them to save time, reduce costs, and achieve higher growth. Embracing innovation would enable an organization to increase its chances of profitability and enhance its competitive edge over rivals. In addition to the above advantages, leaders should consider it a huge responsibility to conduct an analysis of the market environment, that is, the customer's needs and competitor's strategies. Being open to new ideas and adaptive to change, and identifying, evaluating, and exploiting new technologies is another way of embracing innovation strategies in making operations and processes faster and more effective. Leaders need to seek relevant advice in utilizing available resources, knowing and understanding the current market trends but needing to study the moves of their rivals. There are various ways to embrace innovation and technology, including by developing and implementing effective and realistic strategies with the aim of increasing organizations' capacity and investing more in research and development programmes, which would help identify patterns for discovering, evaluating, and exploiting new technologies effectively and efficiently using lean processes.

In making innovation realistic and acceptable, leaders need to have studied a particular system or process for a specific period to identify the causes of a particular problem, knowing and understanding that the strategic downside of the problem must be addressed. This enables the ability to generate possible ideas of recreating the system or process and making it a vision, which is, seeing the system as effective and applicable from another dimension so as to create another culture within an organization. It is also up to leaders to identify the required drivers for innovation and determine how to make others understand and capture the vision and idea, making it possible for the innovation process to leave a trail to realize opportunities by applying the new idea to work structures. An innovation statement needs to be developed so as to identify blockages to innovation and to determine how best to overcome the barriers to innovation. Afterwards, leaders can measure the impact of going with the final decision or not going with it. If the new system is acceptable, it's advisable to prioritize innovation at this stage to ensure those with the highest impact are realized first. As a matter of fact, innovation and creativity could be applied for the purpose of developing effective strategy and detailed implementation plans that would ensure the successful execution of the new idea, and lastly identify the benefits of innovation as a whole.

SUSTAINABILITY

In general, sustainability is based on a simple principle—the ability or capacity of something to be maintained and sustained over a period of time, such as an organization's reputation. It's paramount to understand that leaders who embrace sustainability record long-term success because it prevents the organization from being liquidated. However, everything humans need for survival depends, either directly or indirectly, on the natural environment. In a nutshell, leaders need to embrace sustainability to avoid waste of current resources for the benefit of the future. Sustainability creates and maintains the conditions under which an organization can exist in productive harmony with stakeholders, which allows fulfilling the social, economic, and other requirements of present and future generations. Sustainability is important to making sure those human needs such as water, materials, and resources, that is, those things that protect human health and the environment as a whole, continue to be available.

Sustainability is maintaining organizational resources rather than depleting or destroying them. A deep understanding of sustainability enables leaders to identify those actions and activities that could help provide an insight of how be best to achieve the maximum resources being invested for the purpose of profitability. Sustainability involves incorporating social, economic, and environmental factors into an organization's strategic planning process so as to facilitate perfect decisions, but it also about connecting and interacting with society in order to recognize the impact of their presence as stakeholders towards community development and benefits. Sustainability is also a platform for organizations to negotiate their interdependence to operate within the environment without any form of harm or sanctions. Sustainability, as a matter of fact, is as much about exchanging value towards others in all undertakings and commitment for the sake of peace as it is about upholding a good reputation. However, without the environment, neither business nor community could exist; therefore, leaders need to see sustainability as a strategic imperative for organizational growth. It's wise for leaders to focus on making long-term goals realistic rather than making short-term profit for the purpose of achieving organizational sustainability.

If an organization is trying to do more than necessary, there is a huge tendency to fall short of the required resources to execute strategic plans over the long term. Another major aspect in ensuring an organization becomes and remains sustainable is the ability of leaders to have a realistic vision and viable goals for their organizations. Furthermore, the main goal of having a sustainable organization is to achieve a good financial reserve and also have the capabilities to execute contingency planning. However, sustainable organizations prove to be more profitable as they adapt and grow with the changing market, aiming at having a better competitive advantage within the industry.

For any leader to achieve a better level of sustainability within a reasonable time frame, he needs to identify, understand, and know how to implement the key to a successful sustainability plan, given the available resources and the cost for executing an organizational strategic plan. The key to a successful sustainability plan includes: creating a plan, building a powerful team, remaining in control, implementing strategic plans, and monitoring outcomes.

In most cases, the budget of an organization might prevent a full-throttle commitment to changes necessary to reach certification levels of sustainability. However, sustainable leadership means planning and preparing for succession in terms of service and operational delivery. It's also about setting a realistic strategy in place to accomplish goals, which inspires and empowers others towards productivity.

The following plan, while not all inclusive, can get a company started on the right track. As the changes and sustainability efforts begin to save the company money, funds can be directed into a more comprehensive sustainability plan.

1. CREATING A PLAN

This first part of sustainability includes the required processes and actions an organization needs to take to maximize its chances for survival, and perhaps even to thrive, despite the level of uncertainty that might occur in the future. This plan is a concrete process that an organization takes on course for several months in terms of implementation; it needs to be an on-going process that should become part of an organization's operational system, indicating how best to utilize organizational resources strategically to achieve organizational stability. Having a plan is not the only thing that matters; the plan must be reasonable, applicable, and implementable, having a specific intention and being attainable within an expected timeframe.

Leaders need to ensure that others are committed to the succession of the plan so that it is attainable without involving unnecessary stress. As a matter of fact, leaders need to understand the role of communication and involvement, which are key factors in the issue of the stakeholders' relationships.

Planning plays a huge role in sustainability and productivity because it consists of forecasting, decision-making, and problem-solving. However, decision-making is an important part of planning because it requires leaders to make the right decisions at the right time to the benefit of the organization. According to Koontz and O'Donnell, planning is "deciding in advance what we want to do, how to do it, when to do it, and who will do it. Planning bridges the gap from where we are to where we want to go. It makes it possible for things to occur which would not otherwise happen." In the real sense of it, where we want to go is a serious parameter that determines who, when, and how to do something, which creates more advantages for an organization because it enables leaders to pay more attention to desired objectives to minimize uncertainty and risk. Planning improves the efficiency of operations by avoiding confusion and chaos. Other benefits of planning are that it encourages innovation and creativity while also facilitating cooperation and team work. However, there is always a downside: planning could be negatively affected by some unfortunate situations, including the lack of accurate information, taking too much time, shortage of recourses for implementation, rigidity due to strict compliance with plans, a psychological barrier or unwillingness of people to change, changes in government policies, technology, labour unions, market conditions, competitors' actions, or natural calamities. It's possible to overcome the barrier of planning by developing clear-cut objectives and better forecasting, while also having a sound communication system across an organization.

2. BUILDING A POWERFUL TEAM

Team-building is an essential part of an organizational set-up because without it, other resources remain stuck where they are. Team building is the process of motivating and enabling the team to achieve specific goals for the purpose of accountability. Building an effective team is not keeping an organization at its peak; rather, it is the ability to maintain the team spirit and dynamics over a long period. The stages of team-building include the ability of leaders to clarify the team goals, build a good level of understanding, create ownership to act without any form of fear, remove inhibitors, introduce enablers, and use processes to move up the ladder of performance.

Team-building activities are useful for improving team dynamics, building trust, facilitating communication, and creating better relationships and teamwork. However, the foundation of good teamwork is having a shared commitment towards achieving specific objectives.

Team-building is not just a single event that can be done by someone outside the team; it's a task primarily for the team leaders and the team members themselves. However, in order to build a powerful team, and get their support, it's better for leaders to set smaller goals in the beginning that can easily be achieved and then reward everyone's efforts the same way. Leaders need to be realistic with their formation and execution processes because those two reflect their capability to handle the team in any situation. Strong teams that are inclusive, outward facing, and performance oriented have the essentials for transforming an organization into a positive force for society and the environment.

In order to keep up the momentum, leaders should build a centralized team, making them represent all aspects of an organization. Building a strong team encourages multi-disciplinary work where teams cut across organizational divides; it also fosters flexibility and responsiveness, especially the ability to respond to change.

3. REMAINING IN CONTROL

Once a team has been established and cost-saving strategies are in place, leaders should expand their horizons by seeking new ideas on how to keep an organization ahead in terms of the competition by attending sustainability programs at various business seminars/events, professional institutes, or coaching seasons that specialize in helping an organization to become greener. The more knowledge an organization gives its employees, the more eager they will be to help the organization reach its goals. Being in control of a team is not a matter of a leader being bigger than the team they lead or having arrogant behaviour towards their members. It's not a matter of having the whole say, but rather a matter of tendering issues on board before making decisions that need to be applied and then standing by them. It's important to make clear rules and sanctions for the behaviour of team members, and leaders need to respect those rules themselves.

4. DEVELOP AND IMPLEMENT STRATEGIC PLANS

Developing an actionable strategic plan revolves around proper design. However, having developed a strategic plan, a leader should determine a sustainable design process and identify a realistic time for anticipated achievement to give elements of quality in terms of performance. Developing and implementing strategic plans might require hiring an external consultant to have some new ideas of how to get things done, rather than sticking to the old ways of doing things. It's paramount at this stage for leaders to involve the relevant people and gather the necessary inputs for those who will help implement the plan. Next, break the plan into tasks. While the plan needs to contain large, long-term goals, it is equally important to develop actionable steps for achieving them. It's also better to be realistic about what is achievable based on the size and strength of organizational resources and the supporting team. Having a dream is not all that is required for success—it's also knowing how best to implement strategies that have a lot to do with time and situation, especially when the strategy is new. Some helpful activities for implementing the strategic plan in terms of sustainability include assigning tasks with due dates and applying effective control measures. Distributing a plan in a format that is easy to understand and conducive to implementation, given that the leader knows the skills of his or her team, is another way of making a strategic plan realistic.

Leaders should consider it paramount to see strategic planning as a platform that gives the opportunity to make key decisions in line with their organizational purpose, that is, what matters most at a particular time or the problem that needs to be tackled. The beauty of every implementation process is the quality of the problem it solves. In the sense of productivity, leaders need to encourage every stakeholder to understand the nature of the problems an organization is facing and how crucial they are, especially in terms of potential impact on the organization not being addressed in a timely manner, and the need to come up with new strategies for the best solutions.

5. MONITORING OUTCOMES

Both in theory and in practice, monitoring and evaluating activity has a huge purpose in sustaining an organization. However, leaders need to place great importance on these because, when done and used in the right manner, it strengthens the basis for managing the results, fosters learning and knowledge generation within an organization, and knocks down the barriers and forces against development. In a nutshell, conducting a periodic review of the sustainability plan is important so that adjustments can be made. In keeping good communication with employees, a company may discover that small adjustments are necessary and applicable. The purpose of outcome monitoring is to continually and systematically track internal performance metrics across an organization. Monitoring as a whole helps leaders test sustainability on various criteria such as: Evaluation, which helps focus more on the standards against which organizational activities would be would assessed; Relevance, which helps in determining the extent to which an initiative is consistent and responsive to national and local policies and priorities of stakeholders; Effectiveness, which is a measure of the extent to which an initiative's intended results (outputs or outcomes) have been achieved or the extent to which progress toward outputs or outcomes has been achieved; Efficiency, which measures how economically resources or inputs (such as funds, expertise, and time) are converted to results; and Impact, which measures changes in human development and people's wellbeing that are brought about by development initiatives, directly or indirectly, intended or unintended.

As a matter of fact, major challenges facing organizations in term of sustainability have been the ability to accelerate the pace for improvement and the ability to participate actively in partnerships and networks that can create an increased capacity for more sustainable development.

Sustainability measures the extent to which initiatives continue to benefit all involved stakeholders at a particular period of time. However, assessing sustainability involves evaluating the extent to which relevant social, economic, political, institutional, and other conditions are present and, based on that assessment, making projections about the organizational capacity to maintain, manage, and ensure the required developments occur in the future.

In summary, sustainability strategy, including the development of key stakeholders, should be considered and implemented knowing the financial stability of the organization, resources, systems, and structures. It has to be in accordance with relevant policies and regulatory frameworks that are in place so as to support continuous benefits for an organization as a whole. In everyday life, sustainability can be achieved by reducing consumption of resources such as water and energy in terms of avoiding waste, increasing the recycling of used materials, and protecting forests and soil all over the earth. However, when most people think of sustainability, they are focusing on corporate responsibility as a business's effect on and relationship which stakeholders. To make the most impact, responsible leaders need to see stakeholders as full partners and meaningful instruments for the evolution of healthier communities and better opportunities.

Having considered the operational needs for productivity, leaders have a huge role to play in establishing a successful and sustainable organization, which takes more than managing the day-to-day operations of the enterprise. It requires genuine leadership, the ability to guide individuals and teams to their highest level of collaboration, innovation, and effectiveness. Today's leadership is about leaders being able to play various roles: visionary, role model, and architect, defender of values, team builder, coach, change agent, strategist, economist, and advocate for excellence. It's not all about profit-making. Leaders need to understand the importance of creating a value-driven vision that can become the benchmark for individual and organizational decision-making. They also need to continuously seek the best practices that can foster higher levels of integrity, adaptability, sustainability, and execution for the main purpose of productivity.

Being productive requires aiming higher with a positive mind and a realistic viewpoint towards achieving greater heights. R. Kelly said in his hit record, "I believe I can fly: if I can see it, then I can do it, if I just believe it, there's nothing to it." I see the self-confidence backing an intention of getting things done, displacing fears and distractions. Productivity in leadership requires equipping oneself with the right skills, knowledge, and understanding because without it, confusion would be the case in teams that handle complex issues. It is all that is required to supply others with the necessary items or conditions either physically or mentally for a particular purpose and task.

THE SEVEN LAWS

THE LAW OF FOCUS

Once lost, a vision ends.

Whenever you want to achieve something, keep your eyes open, concentrate and make sure you know exactly what it is you want. No one can hit their target with their eyes closed.
—Paulo Coelho, The Devil and Miss Prym

Focus is a powerful tool and a major step towards a desired achievement. Once lost it becomes easy to miss one's vision. It is very important to embrace and establish focus in order to remain on course and to attain a desired direction. Regardless of any desired and realistic vision, the ability to remain focused promotes the courage and commitment to carry on, not to mention the rigidity and toughness to achieve it. One can never be an effective leader without focus. Each time I listen to Shania Twain's song "You're Still the One," it makes me understand the importance of being focused on a journey towards success. Being focused requires one to be determined towards an achievement, especially when one seems to be surrounded by impossibilities, obstacles, delays, and discouragement. For one to be focused, a desire for an outstanding outcome must be in place, which requires some level of determination. In turn, this reflects one's seriousness of mind in making a vision a reality. Getting and setting the right direction alongside establishing focus on the right issue within an accurate time frame is what makes a leader realistic. I remember a local boxing competition staging Andrew and Evans, who were both friends of mine during my school days. These childhood friends had trained together for years before departing to different parts of the country due to the progression of their careers. Getting to the sixth round of the competition, Evans had succeeded in gaining points, making use of some advantage of his skills. Everyone thought Andrew was losing it, but Andrew kept on hitting Evans on the left shoulder and began to score more points. All the while, his coach kept shouting, "Focus!" Long story short, Evans later became weak in stretching his right hand and could hardly lift his left. In the tenth round, Andrew began to hit the left shoulder to weaken its strength and later focused on the right. Evans finally gave in and Andrew won. After great joy and excitement from Andrew's fans, he later said in an interview that the moment he remembered Evans was right handed, he began to focus more on weakening it to reduce his strength, which enabled him to achieve his desire.

THE LAW OF FOCUS

> The key to success is to focus our conscious mind
> on things we desire, not things we fear.
> —Brian Tracy

Taking insight from that Brian Tracy's quote, the key to success is focus, in the real sense of it. No one ever achieves anything without being focused. It's the next step, having gotten a determined mind to achieve long-term and reasonable goals. The main reason for desiring achievement is to stand out in one's world among others, but either one gets it done or ditches it. Determination on its own is similar to a bulldozer smashing down walls that seem to be an obstacle towards achieving the desired success that is, giving what it takes to get things done. Long-term achievements require a conscious mind, a vital element that strengthens one's determination and focus towards achievements, else it becomes so easy for anyone to become weary and give out before the triumphant moment. A focused leader would remain in the light of what he or she wants and would keep doing this regardless of the situation surrounding the resources at hand. Capitalizing less on fears and more on one's strength to promote one's ability to bring out one's best to achieve a particular desire reflects focus in any leader. "We knew we'd get there someday," is a statement that reflects the hope and courage of any potential achiever and focused person. It requires believing in one's ability by having a positive mind towards making a vision realistic no matter what it takes. Focus is a matter of how well and not how far, because how well is quality in context of an output while how well is merely quantity. Focus is about doing one thing at a time.

The secret of any effective leader is the ability to combine priority and concentration with focus. A leader may be well aware of his priorities but has no concentration; he knows what to do, but he will never finish anything on time or might never finish anything at all. On the other hand, if a leader has concentration but does not know his priorities, she might get things done but find himself or herself constantly off track due to lack of concentration. However, a leader who learns and develops these key characteristics will have the potential and ability to accomplish great things over a long period. Daniel Goldman describes the three levels of focus:

- Inner focus, which is a limitation of self-awareness and self-management: the act of being realistic in tuning in to our guiding values, knowing what we capable of achieving, aiming for objectives with the available skills and resources, and backed with self-confidence and positive emotions. Inner focus makes it possible and easier to turn around situations when facing obstacles and setbacks. It helps in resetting one's platform, especially when adjustment becomes necessary in avoiding defeat. Inner focus promotes the ability to get things done by making situations clearer and highlighting where to lay more emphasis to overcome unpleasant situations. Inner focus attunes us to our emotions and intuitions, guiding values, and better decisions.
- Other focus describes how well we attune to people: our empathy, which allows us to

understand how people perceive things, how they feel, and what we can do to help them be at their best. And tuning in to others this way provides the basis for skill in competencies like motivating employees, persuasion and influence, negotiation and conflict resolution, and, increasingly important, teamwork and collaboration. "Other" focus is a platform in driving towards a specific direction, having shown the big picture via effective communication. The other focus smoothens our connections to the people in our lives.

- Outer focus has to do with how well we can sense the large forces that shape our world, whether organizational dynamics, like whose opinion matters most for a decision; economic forces, such as how a new technology will roil a market; or environmental trends, like the new value placed on lower-carbon processes. Outer awareness allows a leader, for example, to formulate a winning strategy that anticipates what's coming. For any leader to attain a better position within any given industry he or she must focus on external trends, otherwise it is going to be easy to be displaced by rivals. Outer focus lets us navigate the larger world.

Without focus as a whole, it's impossible for any leader to be productive. However, it is important for anyone to focus their time, energy, and effort on one thing at a time for the purpose of clarification of objectives to produce tremendous results. In the reality of it, being focused is not all about the availability to execute a particular task, but having the required concentration to identity the major issue to be hammered out, reflecting active participation in making accurate decisions and having less conversation in achieving expected results. Focus creates effective and competent leaders who reach their peak potential and spend more time fixating on what they do best rather than struggling with their weakness. Leaders should learn to set their priorities straight by delegating some tasks to save time and energy towards execution. As leaders, it is paramount to learn to attack their fears by taking encouraging steps with a positive mind and never see challenges as unrealistic. Being focused is the major parameter in setting goals and directions for an organization as well as building the capability and talent for an organization. It also requires that leaders ensure that stakeholders understand how their work relates to the organization's mission, having known and understood it. Focus requires leaders to believe in what they are doing before they can achieve goals.

Focus is more than a word; it's a necessity in everyday phenomena in areas of one's professional career, family, health, and finances. Focus is a gentle yet powerful skill that enables leaders to tap into the wisdom required to make positive changes within an organization.

Effective leaders need to open their minds and stay focused on the outcomes they wish to achieve. However, they also need to familiarize themselves with the applicable strategies to achieve them. Focus requires leaders to continuously emphasize the relevance and importance of their organizational mission, vision, values, and strategic goals for others to follow in providing direction and structure. Focus in leadership as a whole enables leaders to identify and meet the future challenges of an organization and determine the best way to face them. Organizational challenges include the need for development for the purpose of high potential across the organization's units in order to maintain the best position possible within any industry. The perfect implementation of strategic plans requires leaders to be more focused on determining parameters that could facilitate the smooth running of operational processes of each unit within an organization—"birds of a feather flock together"—and this is the main reason leaders should focus on operational units and components, to avoid an overall breakdown leading to setbacks in meeting the market needs. Another need to focus on implementation of strategic plans is to identify possible measures for improvements aimed at facing down the forces against change within an organization.

For any leader and organization to reflect productivity, there is a significant requirement to focus on the needs of customers by making sure their needs are primary in all their activities, developing and sustaining productive and better customer relationships and other forms of strategic alliances for the future of the organization. Leaders need to draw a platform that quickly and effectively solves customer problems, which shows responsiveness to customers' objectives and needs. Focus remains a powerful driver towards excellence and brings more results when maintained at its peak. Combined with the right training, skills, and knowledge, one would get to his destination quicker than if he or she had not been distracted.

Anyone who can take control of his ability to focus and block out distractions will have a powerful tool to create the platform for consistent, high-level performance. Focus is what determines and sets the yardstick for both effectiveness and efficiency in a workplace, in which the result is always: better quality work, additional success, and achievement of both personal and organizational goals.

A certain man who was trying to avoid borrowing money from the local shylock went to get an interest-free loan from a long-time friend. Rather than focusing on the purpose of his visit, he went on to discuss sports, politics, and history. Meanwhile, another man came to visit the same friend. His friend excused him to attend to the other man. Upon the friend's return, the man brought up the purpose of his visit, but it was too late—the other man was also in need of money, and he got the friend's money first by not beating around the bush. Although the man almost reached his goal, he couldn't close the transaction. He could have achieved the purpose of his visit, but he lacked focus and didn't bring up the right issue at the right time. He ended up getting a loan from the shylock and paid a high interest rate simply because he lacked focus on what he wanted at his friend's place.

It's wiser to focus on one thing at a time. Doing many things at a time makes one a jack of all trades, master of none. I remember a lady crossing a busy road and sending a text at the same time to her boyfriend. Being focused requires discipline and determination, which can't be neglected when trying to achieve an excellent performance and a greater result.

Leaders need to focus by taking an in-depth view into

the situation before making a decision, else, there would be a huge need for reversing decisions after time, money, and energy were wasted. Leaders need to understand that a particular solution can never be applicable for all problems because some require a higher level of experience and maturity to handle. However, leaders need to be focused from the present into the future, that is, the current state of an organization to the desired state, and to remain on course towards an agreed direction.

The value of being focused lies in the achievement of a leader, which makes his story worth hearing because no one ever wants to embrace or invest in failure. A perfect point to enhance productivity in leadership is for organizations to focus more on solutions rather than the problem. Outsourcing experts could most times save the cost of handing problematic situations repeatedly, provided an expectation had been accepted and agreed on. In the meantime, time, money, and energy could be invested in other things.

THE LAW OF COMMITMENT

Without it, success remains impossible.

With a powerful desire, with strong determination, and with a commitment to yourself, you can find ways to achieve your goals and overcome challenges.
—Catherine Pulsifer

There's no abiding success without commitment.
—Anthony Robbins

I wish someone could tell me a success story without reflecting commitment towards achieving it, or show a leader with much potential and credibility without commitment. Commitment is a continuous process of being focused towards an achievement. It is one thing to have a nice dream or vision and another to achieve it, which requires commitment. A speaker said at a conference how the late musical legend Michael Jackson would spend more than ten hours a day rehearsing dance steps alone. Commitment evokes a strong sense of intention and focus because it facilitates taking steps. It typically is accompanied by a statement of purpose or a plan of action also serving as the backbone and driving force of achievement, which makes it more meaningful. In general, people who are seriously committed don't give up. They believe in what they are doing by remaining focused, tolerant, and perseverant for the purpose of success. Commitment is the continuous process of being focused. It's therefore to be taken seriously by any leader.

The story of ten virgins in the Bible reflects those who are serious in seeing the bridegroom by fuelling their lamp with the right quality at the right time. Commitments are important in ensuring that leaders achieve their desired outcome while investing resources such as time, energy, and money for organizational productivity. However, it reflects how determined, prepared, and serious someone is towards his or her achievements. Commitment is required in pursuing organizational goals consistently while applying control measures to compare both actual and standard results. It's also required in applying creativity, ingenuity, and resourcefulness to resolving problems or issues that would otherwise block the achievement of the goal. Being committed to positive ideas enables the formulation and development of a realistic strategic framework for execution. Commitment as a whole enables leaders to stand fast in the face of adversity, remaining determined and focused in the quest for the desired goal. Serious commitment is the willingness to sacrifice what it takes or to require turning challenges into steps and climbing them towards the achievement. Committed leaders see difficult situations as stepping stones with a mind of taking responsibility rather than giving an excuse for failure and avoiding taking action where and when necessary. Being committed is a powerful weapon against discouragement and criticism toward being a success. It fosters trust and transparency in one's approach and abilities towards greatest.

Making an investment without being committed towards its success is the best way to waste resources. In simple terms, commitment is an agreement to act because it weighs more than words. Where is there no commitment, there is no activity, no movement, nor motion. A good level of commitment would always make a good mentor and role model for others. It is best demonstrated and proven by a leader's actions on a regular basis; it requires taking a stand in any situation. There is no way a leader can effectively influence others for their support without being committed to the vision of an organization. If a leader acts with determination and commitment, great numbers of people will really pay attention and follow. Leading by example is one good way to reflect commitment because it boosts the confidence of others while an organization passes through hard times. However, it requires commitment for any leader or organization to stand out in terms of performance. Commitment goes along with being focused, confident and self-motivated, which brings the action in any leader. It requires paying attention to the concerns of others.

Commitment grows in a natural way—leaders can foster commitment within an organization by tabulating the reward for hard work as a team, which in turn enhances the willingness and dynamics to focus on achieving excellent results. Examples of growth in the level of commitment within a team include: working and making decisions together, appreciating and respecting each other, building and maintaining relationships, and challenging each other to take steps forward.

Commitment is a chapter of one's mind that requires dedication to accomplish something significant in any field and doesn't usually occur at one moment. It grows over time within an organization. Outputs always reflect how committed leaders have kept to their goals. For commitment to be achieved, both leaders and stakeholders need to build relationships and work together by feeling successful at what they do, that, believes in the win-win factor, making decisions together, and supporting one another, which is the best way to overcome obstacles and work through conflicts. However, it requires commitment to one's desired goal to challenge oneself towards taking the next step in any situation. It gives one the ability to learn from others with the aim of improving, appreciating, and respecting the contributions and efforts of others. Commitment is not all about being punctual for a task, but rather about applying a concentrated and vigorous effort towards accomplishing the same task with a unique result at the end. Perseverance is another issue to be considered in any leader's commitment, especially when passing through adverse conditions, which requires them to be persistent in their activities and not diverting from the major issue at hand. Self-discipline is another reflection of any committed leader because it enables him or her to stand and define what he is responsible for, what he wants at a particular time, where he wants to be, and how to do get things done within an organization. Leaders need to be committed in the development of their staff, especially the frontline staff, because it gives them a good feeling about their contribution and effort and encourages them to become actively involved in the growth of the organization. John Maxwell once said at a particular seminar, "Every good and successful thing begins with commitment; without it, nothing works." Leaders must demonstrate commitment by making specific promises about observable behaviors' within an organization and give realistic and applicable solutions to the problems they discover. Another way of demonstrating commitment is for leaders to be loyal in their relationships with stakeholders and also build operational platforms for effective communication, transparency, competency, and consistency. In a nutshell, commitment has to be nurtured continuously or it will grow stale and wane. It means focusing on the bigger picture and going the extra mile in making sacrifices and delaying gratification in order to invest in the comfort of the future. Commitment to any effective leader means living with integrity by sticking to one's beliefs and values by being honest with oneself and others. It also means continually and deliberately reaching beyond one's comfort zone and doing what others won't in order to achieve one's goal. A committed leader is always ready to go the extra mile in the pursuit of success, regardless of the situation, while others are giving up, because it enables him or her to remain motivated towards taking action, which would at one point or another provides a filter for better opportunities. It becomes easier to overcome resistance once someone is committed to a specific goal because it enables one to see and celebrate progress attained.

Commitment requires the understanding of a leader's strengths and weaknesses and maximizing the former while trying to minimize the latter. Committed leaders never fear taking risks or making errors; rather, they learn from the accompanying mistakes. They believe strongly in fostering collaboration by promoting cooperative goals and building trust, which makes it easier to envision an uplifting and ennobling future for an organization as a whole. However, leaders need to recognize individual contributions to the success of an organization and also celebrate accomplishments regularly.

THE LAW OF AUTHENTICITY

Brings out the real leader in anyone.

Enlightenment is the key to everything, and it is the key to intimacy, because it is the goal of true authenticity.
—Marianne Williamson

The Law of Authenticity is and remains the most valuable gift a leader would ever have to offer himself or herself and others. Leaders who are authentic attract followers, even leaders who are viewed as being highly driven due to the belief they have in themselves. Authenticity provides leaders with the currency to obtain 'buy-in' from key stakeholders, because it builds and maintains trust. Authenticity is the bedrock upon which the other facets are built. Authenticity simply reflects that leaders are being unique and genuine and real, not false, that they are not copying someone else's beliefs and that their actions having been tested and confirmed. It's always impossible for any leader to make a positive impact on others and to be successful without being authentic and productive. Authenticity is an important aspect in leadership; it consists of trust and integrity, which are important components in reflecting how competent a leader is. Stakeholders not only need to know what a leader can achieve, they also need to understand their motives, visions, values, goals, and plans, a typical example of values-based leadership. Authentic leaders are respected and entrusted for their vision because it is believed they genuinely care about what's happening within the organization. This makes them successful and capable of fulfilling their promises. Another reason why authentic leaders are more respected is their consistency in watching out for and maintaining the interests of every stakeholder. An authentic leader needs to be able to hear and incorporate feedback, both good and otherwise, reflecting it as a better listener. The act of being a better listener enables others to see them as being accommodating, transparent, productive, and innovative. Authentic leaders become empowering role models to followers as they lead in a manner that others recognize as authentic.

Team members feel more comfortable in their relationship with authentic leaders, which have important implications for resultant outcomes and performance due to the belief that authentic leaders are naturally multipliers. Authentic leadership is all about helping members recognize potential ways of increasing the effectiveness of talents and skills through an open and honest relationship and nurturing those talents and skills into strengths. Nothing makes it possible for anyone to leave a legacy for others to follow more than being authentic, because an authentic leader's impact lives forever in the hearts of the those around her and through other generations. Winston Churchill will never be forgotten in the history of Britain because of his courageous actions and leadership during World War II. Being authentic is one of the major pillars of success without any doubt due to its wonderful significance, which makes it better for any leader to possess. On the other hand, copycats are pretenders and failures regardless of their sweet excuses. Authentic leaders are constantly building their legacies by adding deep value to everyone that they deal with and leaving the world a better place in the process.

> The keys to brand success are self-definition, transparency, authenticity, and accountability.
> —Simon Mainwaring

There is nothing more to effective leadership than the above quote by Simon Mainwaring, who happens to an award-winning branding consultant. Authentic leaders need to see themselves as role models with a legacy to pass on to the upcoming generation. However, authentic leaders need to constantly build their legacies by adding deep value to everyone that they deal with. They need to be committed to excellence rather than perfection, which can be achieved only by having respect for the views and ideas of others around them for solutions, because no man is an island of knowledge. However, no human being is perfect. Authentic leaders know themselves intimately; they know their weaknesses and play to their strengths and also spend a lot of time transcending their fears regardless of what comes their way. An authentic leader needs to be courageous because it requires courage to be a visionary and stick to what is right. They speak their truth and lead from their heart at all times. For leaders to be and remain authentic, they need to possess a wealth of knowledge, experiences, and insight on how best to lead others and make them grow. Transparency in leaders makes them discuss their thoughts openly, which makes them achieve high levels of trust and commitment in terms of support from others. Accountability is another aspect of leadership that makes a leader authentic. It serves as the guiding principle that defines how commitments are being made towards each other in the form of stewardship, which makes leaders responsible for the success or failure of an organization.

Being authentic as a leader encourages stakeholders to remain open, honest, and direct in their relationships and transactions while also giving valuable and continuous feedback. Another benefit of authenticity is that it helps build trust and confidence in stakeholders. It becomes easier to know and understand one's stand regarding an issue. Being authentic makes a leader's actions relevant, realistic, and reasonable in the sight of stakeholders.

Leaders with authentic behaviors' are more accessible than many believe because they are being honest by speaking the truth. They are often known for hitting the nail on the head, not beating around the bush, and being direct by making their actions and words clear, concise, and focused. They are also non-judgmental of others; they only speak about what they are experiencing within an organization and around others, not hiding from facts and realities.

It all lies in the hands of an authentic leader to help an organization drive a culture of excellent results and sustainability through effective leadership. Bill George's book Authentic Leadership: Rediscovering the Secrets to Creating Lasting Value makes it clear that authentic leaders need to demonstrate a passion for their purpose, practice their values consistently, and lead with their hearts as well as their heads. Authentic leaders need to act as a catalyst for change within their organizations to stimulate growth. Authenticity enables leaders to always be the object and never the shadow by creating a realistic vision and value congruence across team members and an organization as a whole. It helps to foster higher levels of both organizational commitment and productivity.

A successful leader makes a continuous effort to learn and practice new skills, which is a reflection of commitment. Leadership requires commitment, which includes being a good listener before talking and taking action while taking the emotional feelings of others into consideration. However, authentic leaders possess insight that helps in making vision real and create a better platform for wisdom for the demonstration of initiative. They exude influence and manifest with integrity.

THE LAW OF CONSISTENCY

Little steps, huge impact.

Success is neither magical nor mysterious. Success is the natural consequence of consistently applying basic fundamentals.
—Jim Rohn

Let there be consistency in whatever you do and whatever you say. If what you think and say is mismatching with what you do, you can't really be trusted.
— Israel more Ayivor, Shaping the Dream

Little drops make a mighty ocean, but it is always as a result of consistency and maintaining a better focus in a certain and specific direction. The Law of Consistency says that "motivation gets you going – discipline keeps you growing," according to John C. Maxwell in his book The 15 Invaluable Laws of Growth: Live Them and Reach Your Potential. Without consistency, a leader keeps on telling the same old story, that is, there is stagnancy and no improvement. Studying the same law of consistency, according to John Maxwell, for any leader to be successful, he or she needs to be consistent, to clear the air, and to understand the impact of discipline in achieving goals. Achieving goals at specific periods is the major parameter that changes the story of a leader and makes her worthwhile. As such, consistency is very important in leaders because it creates stability and trust in the stakeholders' perception of them.

A good leader is always consistent in seeking various ways for improvement, which requires the utilization of specific learning and impacting resources or finding a mentor or coach to help navigate one's path and steps to improve. Consistency is a single standard policy, not a matter of A today, B tomorrow. Improving one's skills and ability requires developing a plan and laying a solid foundation. Most importantly, leaders need to be patient and value the process attained. It requires consistency to persuade others effectively because one's audience would know and trust one's ability. Consistency makes it easy to develop one's potential talent. Dr Maxwell made it clear in his book: Talent is never enough; it's hard to succeed without talent and without being consistent in developing that same talent, it's similar to tea without sugar. Consistency plays a huge role in the life of a leader by enabling him to believe in succeeding at what he is doing and wanting to achieve by not giving up. Consistency enables a leader to build and rely on courage in facing challenges while pursuing his or her passions in combination with his or her talent. This takes continuous practice and improvement and requires leaders to remain focused and open to suggestions.

While making all reasonable efforts towards both individual and organizational success, leaders much absolutely consider consistency when formulating and executing strategic plans due to their huge importance. The credibility of strategic planning, implementation, and execution depends on how consistent and competent the leaders are.

Consistency is important for all levels of an organization. Without consistency, an organization's mission statement would be regarded without substance or importance. Effectiveness and efficiency are both outcomes of a consistent leadership that facilitates recognition in leaders' activities because consistent leaders consider it paramount to treat everyone fairly and equally.

There are five major components leaders need to ensure to be and remain consistent; otherwise they could find themselves off track.

1: LEADING TO ENHANCE EXCELLENT PERFORMANCE

Leadership as a whole requires building trust, being consistent, and helping others be the best they can be. Leading to enhance performance is never a one-man game but a collective effort that facilities the act of moving from contributing to an organization as an individual or as a manager to being a leader, which requires a shift in thinking and in skills. It's also about clarifying the roles and responsibilities of managing and leading within an organization, allowing each person to know and understand what is expected of them. The major reason leaders need to enhance performance is to help their organizations stay visible and viable and to maintain a good competitive edge over its rivals. Identifying the right initiative in recognizing the current strengths and abilities for leadership positions within any industry as a whole is another reason for leaders to enhance performance. In seeking peak performance, leaders need to communicate their desired expectations and emphasize personal accountability. Monitoring and evaluating job performance at regular intervals is another way to remain on course in teams of leading effectively. Leading by setting a positive example is the best way to inspire results. John Baldoni, author of Lead by Example: 50 Ways Great Leaders Inspire Results, emphasizes that managers who engage in active listening, respect the unique talents of their staff, install confidence in others and know both when and how to delegate responsibilities achieve better results than egotistical leaders who believe that theirs is the only "right" way to get anything done.

2: SETTING CLEAR EXPECTATIONS

One of the key components to effective leadership is the ability of leaders to set expectations for their followers and hold them accountable for their actions. Leaders need to make sure that their vision and expectations are stated repeatedly for others to get the big picture, according to Kevin Eikenberry, the founder of a leadership and learning consulting company. He provides some major steps for setting perfect expectations in his article, including making the expectations clear for oneself, identifying and understanding the purpose of the expectation, and getting an agreement and commitment from followers before making the expectations a reality.

Setting clear expectations gives guidance and enables others to have in-depth insight of what's expected of them and the overall criteria for success. They want to see how and where their jobs fit in and contribute to the big picture and how their work objectives can mesh with their personal goals. Clear expectations are guidance for an organization's strategic planning process, which defines overall direction and objectives. It supports and facilitates an effective communication strategy that tells every member where their impact is required to make organizational strategy a reality, that is, translating plans to actions or accomplishments.

3: COACHING AND GIVING FEEDBACK

Good performance always occurs through supporting others, not by magic. Coaching is a learning process that is aimed at improving the performance of others. People need to be encouraged to learn new habits of success and improve their self-image and self-confidence. Leaders need to know what works well and what needs improvement by understanding the cause of the problem. In order to be helpful, feedback must be specific, immediate, and respectful. Coaching is a very useful and powerful approach used in clarifying needs and goals; it then promotes action to accomplish personal, team, and/or organizational goals and is also helpful in resolving all kinds of complex problems related to people, relationships, and trust in terms of working together. Coaching is essentially about using effective questioning to help individuals explore and understand themselves and the situations they face. I personally see coaching as a platform for increasing one's personal and collective capacity to become better leaders, managers, and professionals.

Coaching helps increase self-confidence and self-esteem by identifying one's weaknesses and turns them into potential successes having acquired the right skills. However, coaching also serves a number of benefits to an organization in the aspect of higher employee retention, succession planning, full utilization of human resources, and strengthening of organizational culture, ethics, and values. Coaching creates better chances of attaining goals within an organization due to the increased skill set and knowledge level of the people within the organization. The implementation of coaching within an organization is a great contribution to the overall development at both the individual and the organizational levels. Coaching is more about asking the right questions and giving the platform for a perfect approach.

4: FOLLOWING UP ON PERFORMANCE COMMITMENTS

Despite a leader's best efforts, there is a need to check how well expectations are being met. It's the leader's major responsibility to identify and understand the problem and identify why expectations are not being met, having clarified expectations to those who are executing organizational strategies and implementing operational processes. A leader also seeks a mutual understanding about the consequences of such shortcomings; however, this stage involves developing a plan for success that rises from previous experiences.

Following up on performance is part of the improvement process within an organization. The follow-up process needs to focus on progress made irrespective of the corrections and plan developments. An important aspect of following up on performance is the approach that enables stakeholders to understand the value of making improvements and how this benefits the organization in both short- and long-term relationships with them.

5: PLANNING AND SUPPORTING DEVELOPMENT

It is one thing for an organization to succeed, but it is entirely another for the same organization to grow, that is, attain various level of success. However, without the required set of knowledge and skills, the story would end similarly to that of a ship that sank in the middle of the ocean. Development plans are essential to guide an organization in skill enhancement and organizational growth. Both leaders and managers need to learn how to use delegation and other on-the job assignments as opportunities to develop others and enable them to grow by knowing how to identify the need for development and making plans to meet those needs by helping others achieve their developmental goals through effective leadership skill. Another reason development is so important is its ability to help an organization achieve economic stability and remove social inequalities whilst protecting and enhancing its values. Leaders need to assess future needs while planning.

The fact is that consistency is the most important

predictor of overall customer experience and loyalty. It is therefore important for leaders and managers to understand why organizations must work continually to provide customers with superior service by having clear organizational policies, rules, and supporting mechanisms to ensure consistency during interaction. Consistency produces stability, which is crucial to facilitate effective leadership within an organization. Consistency enables leaders to set growth-oriented goals and then tracks progress across an organization. Consistency requires leaders to behave, act, and operate with integrity. In short, leadership is all about consistency in any leader within an organization.

Consistency is the major key for achieving real success. It is advisable for leaders to envision it and then build it. However, it also helps in developing a prosperity and positive mindset to overcome challenges in everyday life because it's based on continuous improvement. Consistency is all about trust, which is built by a succession of behaviors', not just words, because behaviors' speak much more loudly than words.

THE LAW OF RESPONSIVENESS

The will to get things done, or ditch it.

Life is 10% what happens to me and 90% how I react.
—John Maxwell

The quality of being responsive or reacting quickly, as a quality in people involves responding with emotion to people and events. Leaders and managers will always find it difficult to communicate, connect, and build relationships with others without exhibiting the act of being responsive. The law of responsiveness enables stakeholders and investors to see both leaders and managers as reliable and trustworthy figures. It requires the act of being responsive to give an organization direction without stakeholders having any form of fear. To overcome the fear of the unknown, leaders need to find their true selves and be responsive in order to successfully face current challenges by stretching their abilities, vision, and team dynamics to experience the best situations later on. It requires responsiveness to transform an organizational performance. A responsive leader is a person who is able to identify both the explicit and implicit needs of others. A responsive leader will always find it easy to identify and know the needs of others and will always be ready to give support in whatever form without giving excuses. Responsive leaders are generally interested and concerned about the wellbeing of their team members. They are more than willing to work together, are less likely to be callous or indifferent, and are always ready to accept responsibility. Their success lies in their ability to earn respect and trust among the people they interact with because it creates a better platform to learn more and generate fresh ideas from each new challenge they face. Their success also has to do with their trust and respect for others, ensuring stakeholders respond positively to any change in programme without any form of fear. There are two major aspects where leaders need to be responsive to keep an organization in a stable position: improving employee productivity. That is, providing accurate and timely information for the purpose of increasing productivity and also avoiding or reducing waste, and maintaining an high level of customer satisfaction. That is, providing accurate and timely information with the aim of providing support to the customer in a more efficient, accurate, and timely manner. However, employee productivity is directly proportional to customer satisfaction. In an organizational context, responsiveness usually means reaction to changing market conditions, competitive threats, or opportunities. It requires leaders to adapt to the evolving environments by changing their execution model where and when necessary. It also means that leaders must constantly strive to stay abreast of the changing needs of stakeholders and situations.

THE LAW OF RESPONSIVENESS

Responsiveness is extremely important in leadership and organizational wellbeing. Being responsive reflects that a leader recognizes the impact and contribution of an organization' steam members, who they need to value to continuously gain the best of their performance via commitment. In a real context, responsiveness in leadership requires leaders to be disciplined, which earns them much respect.

Effective leaders would always consider responsiveness as taking up the challenges to create new opportunities to enhance change, growth, innovation, and improvement within an organization. It's a platform to lead by example and enable others to help others build their confidence, which is a better way of inspiring a shared vision. Knowing what to do and how to get it done but procrastinating all the way is the greatest force against responsiveness, and this problem remains an obstacle to achievement.

THE LAW OF COURAGE

Travelling beyond expectation without a train.

> Success is not final, failure is not fatal: it is the courage to continue that counts.
> —Winston Churchill

According to Dr Maxwell, in his book The 21 Indispensable Qualities of a Leader: Becoming the Person Others Will Want to Follow, one with courage is a majority. Courage enables one to carry on regardless of the disappointment and pain being faced at any moment in one's life. It enables one to remain hopeful of a better future regardless of today's challenges. Courage is a trait that needs to be possessed by all managers and leaders, so much so that leadership that lacks courage is nothing short of a farce. It is simply taking action at the right time, especially when pursuing our dreams regardless of fear and any difficulties one might foresee, and not giving up. Courage is always an important quality of a successful leader. Winston Churchill was prime minister of the United Kingdom from 1940 to 1945 and again from 1951 to 1955. As a former officer in the British Army, he was known for his bravery and was always on the alert for war by giving it what it takes to defend the interests of the British people. He once said, "Courage is what it takes to stand up and speak; courage is also what it takes to sit down and listen."In other words, courage is what it requires to carry others along, especially in tough situations. Courageous leaders believe that: No matter today's outcome, there is always a better tomorrow.

I remember a popular hymn, "Through the Love of God Our Saviour."The first line of the second verse states: "Though we pass through tribulation, all will be well."I see this statement as a courageous one—no matter the obstacles, hindrances, disappointments, and other unpleasant situations being experienced at the moment, the future still remains hopeful and holds the best. Courage is similar to painkillers because it enables one to see an unpleasant existing situation as irrelevant after a while by placing aside any unpleasant situation and simply carrying on. The first line of the third verse of the same hymn is, "We expect a bright tomorrow; All will be well."I see those wording as ones to restore hope. Courage is the foundation that everything is built on. The Bible says, "Weeping may endure for a night, but joy cometh in the morning."

Leaders need to see beyond current situations to remain strong for an expected future, which is achievable if one is focused, committed, and on course towards one's goal.

According to Napoleon Bonaparte, "Courage isn't having the strength to go on, but it's going on when one doesn't have the strength."

No leader is born with strength; rather, it'sbuilt as a result of carrying on when all seems to be gone, which is

THE LAWS OF PRODUCTIVITY

the major role of courage. It requires courage to take responsibility when others are giving excuses, to live with integrity while others are being dishonest, to challenge and change one narrative while others stick to the same old stories, to pursue one's dream while others neglect theirs, to stand and speak up for something while others fall and keep quiet for nothing, to persevere while others quit. Nothing else has ever and would kill fear other than the ability to be and remain brave in taking courageous steps forward, when others are stepping backwards. Life itself is never a smooth journey or a straight-line graph; courage is the only factor that enables us to overcome setbacks and failures that present themselves on the way to our goals, which also brings the greatest sense of achievement and makes our lives worthwhile.

Courage is taking a bold step into action—nothing changes if nothing changes. It requires courage to step out of one's comfort zone in pursuit of greener pastures, and this enables the fulfillment of potential within leaders. Trading procrastination and excuses for a commitment is the only way to be a person who is willing to do what it takes to live one's dream. Regardless of the challenges and contests being faced in one's endeavor, the greatest risk is to do nothing. Fear regret more than failure, for life always rewards action.

However, the challenges facing today's leaders are immense and require great courage to overcome. Leaders are constantly being challenged by stakeholders, such as their team members, customers, or the public. Standing firm in the face of criticism, yet having the courage to admit when things go wrong enables leaders go miles in their careers because those are hallmarks of a courageous

68

leader. Admitting errors or mistakes never indicates failure, but rather creates a better platform for future improvements. Courage is an important virtue of leadership success as a whole. Leaders require courage to make bold decisions even when there are dissenters, to say what needs to be said no matter the consequences, and to place their trust in those they manage. A courageous leader counts it all as joy, bearing pain and inconvenience for the sake of others, which makes it difficult for others to understand them. For successful leaders, courage is a way of life, a habit—I would advise making it a lifelong habit.

It requires courage to make tough decisions by acting the right way regardless of the situation; being courageous or not is always a choice. It's a major step in pursuing our dreams and visions towards becoming successful.

THE LAW OF EMPATHY

Being sensitive and aware of others' feelings.

> I call him religious who understands the suffering of others.
> —Mahatma Gandhi

Leaders are sensitive to and aware of the needs, feelings, and motivations of their people.

Empathy is the capacity for concrete representation of another person's mental state, including the accompanying emotions. Empathy is the ability to see the world as another person, to share and understand another person's feelings, needs, concerns and/or emotional state. My pastor at the youth church used to tell us years ago that we should never treat others the way they wouldn't like to be treated because the way we behave towards other reflects our real person and the way we regard others.

Empathy is a selfless act—it enables one to learn more about people and relationships with people. It is a desirable skill that is beneficial to ourselves, others, and society. Phrases such as 'put yourself in their shoes' imply empathy because they enables leaders to share the feeling of others, especially when making strategic decisions. Empathy simply means demonstrating concern for listening to others' ideas, needs, and feelings, as well as showing a better level of understanding for the purpose of a better and hopeful future.

At first glance, empathy reflects leaders as being democratic because it easy to approach them with any form of fear, which makes it easy to gain their support without stress. However, it is better for leaders to know and understand how others perceive them and to identity the best mode of relationship to operate with, especially in the aspect of dealing with complex challenges or issues that might hinder organizational processes from achieving desired goals.

Leaders can build a sense of trust by strengthening relationships with team members, which is another platform for achieving greater collaboration for improved and continuous productivity.

Empathy allows leaders to create an environment of open communication and more effective feedback because it enables them to understand and explore problems employees face and how to help resolve them.

Being empathetic with others helps leaders to validate what they're going through. It encourages them to understand the root cause behind poor performance and helps others who are struggling to improve and excel. Empathy allows leaders to build and develop better relationships with those they lead. Leaders who lack empathy will end up paying a high price in getting things done because lack of empathy between leaders and their team will eventually lead to the breakdown of relationships, increasing the probability of conflict and possibly facilitating poor decision-making within an organization, which results in losses or less return on the investment of resources.

Instilling a sense of empathy in any leader gives a number of advantages, such as understanding the root cause behind poor performance within an organization and where and how to help struggling team members to improve their ability to excel beyond expectations. Empathy allows leaders to build and develop relationships with those they lead. However, demonstrating empathy in a real sense is a difficult task because it takes time and effort to demonstrate awareness and understanding to know why and how an employee thinks or feels the way he or she does about a particular situation, which is not always easy. Many organizations are focused on achieving goals no matter what the cost to employees.

THE NEED FOR CONTINUOUS IMPROVEMENT

Operational excellence and competitive advantage is the major reason for continuous improvement in any organization. Improved effectiveness is a major parameter that fosters a collaborative work environment. There is a huge need for updated knowledge to develop and facilitate effective leadership within an organization. However, knowledge enables stakeholders to support an organization's mission and remain on course in the initial direction of an organization.

Continuous improvement is a platform for meeting stakeholders' expectations in terms of aligning and prioritizing their wants and needs, which requires effective processes and service approaches in an innovative manner. Stakeholder alignment involves aligning the various needs and wants of key customers, employees, and others. The major priorities of stakeholders are the ability of leaders to be open and honest in terms of dialogue, effectiveness, and decision-making that lead to quality improvements and a common understanding of systems and processes within an organization, measuring what matters and developing quantifiable data and consistent values for decision-making, conceptual and applicable links to strategic planning, and measurable goals for units, departments, and individuals.

In a nutshell, continuous improvement is a method for identifying opportunities for streamlining work and reducing waste. It starts with management, and under their leadership, works down through an organization. Everyone is responsible and has a part to play in making improvements a reality within an organization. Some successful implementations of continuous improvement use the approach known as Kaizen. One of the core principles of Kaizen is self-reflection of processes, which is also known as 'feedback'. The purpose of CIP is the identification, reduction, and elimination of suboptimal processes, in other words, to become efficient. Becoming efficient is achieved through incremental steps or evolutionary change. The marketplace remains competitive, and innovative approaches to getting things done remain a serious issue. In today's business world, multinational companies compete directly against each other, and for the purpose of survival, it is essential that they continually improve their products and customer service.

The aim of organizations operating a continuous improvement system is to improve operational systems within an organization and to create opportunities for further improvement. I would like to analyse how to achieve each of the three Kaizen aspects of continuous improvement, namely, feedback, efficiency, and evolutionary change.

FEEDBACK

Feedback is an essential part of an organizational activity that reflects the outcome of a specific process being implemented, in the relationship of invested input to the output obtained within a time frame. Organizations need to be very sensitive to the variance in quality and quantity of resources employed to obtain various results within different time frames. Feedback helps both leaders and organizations to indicate areas to raise their strengths and to improve, and it also helps to identify actions to be taken to improve performance and stay at the top.

According to mindtools.com, feedback is a two-way street. One needs to know how to give it effectively, and, at the same time, model how to receive it constructively.

Feedback is a powerful tool that helps both leaders and organizations get on track, especially when missing targets. It serves as a guide in assisting in knowing how organizational stakeholders perceive leaders' and managers' performance within a specific duration. Feedback can also be very motivating and energizing. It has strong links to employee satisfaction and productivity.

Feedback is the information leaders need to truly facilitate effectiveness within an organization. In fact, the most effective leaders actively seek feedback to enhance effective performance at all times. It's a better way for leaders to know whether or not an organization is achieving its goals and to understand the importance of various roles and their impact in executing various tasks.

Perfect feedback is goal referenced, tangible, transparent, actionable, timely, ongoing, and consistent. However, stakeholders need to understand the importance, relevance, and expectation of the feedback. It's also wise for managers to turn to a few team members for further discussion on issues related to the feedback, the mind of others, and their thoughts about their performance and ideas to have a clear understanding of the situation and the best alternative measures to solve the problem. Never should a manager or leader treat feedback as a small issue or take it for granted. The fact remains that feedback should always take a flexible approach, and leaders need to accept and motivate others to take the outcome from feedback and value the contributions of members. They should also make sure that effective communications and relationships are maintained for strategic purposes.

EFFICIENCY

Identification of issues is not all that is required for a leader to become efficient; in addition, the leader must have the ability to identify and apply improvement measures in attaining and remaining at his or her peak at all times. The major purpose of efficiency is to reduce or eliminate the problem, thereby also reducing waste to make the change more meaningful.

In most organizations, evolution needs to take place to allow continuous improvement in the aspects of strategic planning and implementation. This helps to strengthen the collective ability of an organization by reaping and applying the benefits of learning innovative approaches for production, making resources available that will enable members to improve continuously over the long run.

The desire for efficiency enables an organization to

create an environment in which it is possible and easy for continuous growth to occur. This environment focuses on achieving strategic objectives and getting things done in the correct manner. Efficiency essentially denotes how well an organization utilizes resources. There is no way leaders could be successful and productive without taking the time to research and break down a project into basic steps in order to achieve success consistently, which reflects efficiency and value for money.

EVOLUTIONARY CHANGE

Evolutionary change occurs over time to ensure the survival of the organization in a fast-changing world, one in which it's easier and more possible for competitors to edge out an organization, especially when change is not being embraced or comes along too late. The speed-up of technology in the introduction of new products to carry out functions faster than ever has become the latest method for organizations to introduce new products. This pushes customers to change their taste and acquire the latest devices to remain in line with the latest fashion. However, leaders need to become familiar with the latest technologies and new ideas in getting things done faster and also to empower and enlighten stakeholders to take such steps in order for the change to have a positive impact on the organization as a whole. It's important for leaders to provide the necessary resources such as training and coaching for others to engage in the evolutionary change process. The unchangeable fact is that organizations must evolve in order to survive, to maintain competitive advantages, because without them, an organization will succumb to the wave of creative destruction of the competition. Leaders need to understand the role of strategy in insuring that organizational evolution is made a reality, because it enables an organization to have a position within any industry.

The achievement of continuous improvement requires a long-term view and the support of all stakeholders. Continuous improvement activities need to be on present in personnel training, periodical review by management, effective resource allocation, realistic and applicable measurement of performance and expectation, and reward and incentive systems for successful adoption of the change process for the purpose of improvements. Continuous improvement is about the willingness to provide the required support and activities to recognize achievements. It is desirable to formulate reasonable and attainable goals relevant to the available time and resources to accomplish them. These goals need to be tangible to give members of the organization something to strive for, with the recognition of helping to maintain their interest and morale. However, leaders need to know and understand the six steps to continuous improvement, which are: (1)identifying the organizational goals that need to be valued, (2) articulating multiple measurable objectives for each goal, (3)selecting and determining appropriate approaches to assess how well objectives are being met, (4)selecting appropriate measures which can be administered, analyzed, and interpreted for continuous improvement, (5) communicating assessment findings to relevant stakeholders involved in the process to deal with hindrances, and (6) using the information from the feedback exercise to make changes.

STEP ONE: IDENTIFYING GOALS

A goal is a statement expressing the ideal intention of an organization within a specific period. In identifying and setting goals, leaders need to capture the required knowledge, skills, and values in transforming an organization to a better state that it was previously in. In a nutshell, goals reflect the actual intention of an organization.

Organizational goals are the ends an organization seeks to achieve its existence and operation. A goal needs to be predetermined and describe possible approaches in which future results and achievements will be attained and toward which present efforts are directed. However, goals are designed to give an organization a favorable public image, provide legitimacy, and justify its activities.

Goals serve as guidelines for action, directing, and channeling employee efforts. They provide parameters for strategic planning, allocating resources, and identifying development opportunities. They provide the constraints for an organization on how to achieve expectations and carry stakeholders along, which is one of the major responsibilities of organizational leaders to encourage. A goal defines the standards of expected performance and makes it easier for leaders to apply the applicable control measures to meet customers and other stakeholders' needs. Additionally, goals help in setting standards for evaluation and also indicate the possible approaches in facing down challenges in tough times.

Goals need to be set and agreed upon by coalitions of stakeholders, who make it possible to fix the right direction for an organization. Goals must be in the interests of all and not favour one group over another. Leaders need to understand that clear goals help others immensely in understanding the task at hand, measuring the results, and achieving success. It's important for leaders to measure organizational progress and seek advice throughout the pursuit of the goal. Leaders should avoid adding too much complexity to the desired goal, as this will have a negative impact on morale, productivity, and motivation.

STEP TWO: IDENTIFY OBJECTIVES

This is the process of breaking down and redefining broad goals by expressing in smaller term show goals are being achieved at the unit level, which allows leaders to identify where initial adjustments are required.

Objectives are the ends that an organization sets out to achieve and that enable leaders to formulate plans to achieve these ends. The major reason to have an objective is to have the parameters for both current and future improvements. Objectives enable organizations to enhance efficiency, productivity, and sustainability of resources whilst reducing waste. It is wise of any organization to continuously set the objective of being and remaining a market leader because it plays a huge role in satisfying all stakeholders. This objective will set the stage to benefit all stakeholders because customers will receive high-quality products, shareholders will receive high dividends, and employees will receive good wages, and so on.

Examples of some of the objectives that improve performance and customer services are minimizing operating costs, minimizing distribution costs, improving operating cycle time, streamlining information technology, and increasing market share and sales.

STEP THREE: SPECIFY APPROACHES

In general, approaches could be defined as a set of procedures by which information is gathered and measured, making use of various instruments and parameters to provide data for various purposes. In most cases, it called management policies. Applying approaches in different situations requires different information and methods to handle various tasks. Organizations need to adopt multiple approaches to seek performance improvement at regular intervals. Leaders need to acquire the required knowledge of the specified approaches and the main techniques for the measurement and quantification of operational risk and their relative merits and drawbacks. The same knowledge of the adopted approaches would help leaders to understand the best governance structures, systems, procedures, and cultural aspects necessary for an organization to successfully manage its activities and minimize operational risk. The objective of having a better approach is to add maximum sustainable value to the activities of an organization. In addition, having a better approach enables leaders to handle change resulting from complexity, innovation, or technology effectively for the purpose of development and implementation of the organization's strategy, the aim of which is to increase the level and quality of productivity over the long run. Nothing else distinguishes an organization from others within the same industry more than adopting suitable approaches, that is, strategy that makes it possible through cost, leadership, differentiation, or focus. However, an organization must make decisions regarding its core competence, mission and high-level goals and objectives, reflecting the reason for selecting a specific approach.

The specific adopted approaches need to describe how an organization's different functions, such as marketing, finance, and operations, that is, its strategic planning, will be able to support the service concept, or meet its targets.

An important aspect of adopted approaches is the tactical execution, which involves the day-to-day activities required to function and support the service strategy. Tactical execution enables an organization to meet its overall objective from the unit level. Without tactical execution, it's difficult for an organization to function because top management depends on the output, or the gathered information, for the purpose of decision-making. Tactical execution includes operations scheduling, staffing, and productivity improvement, which goes a long way towards determining the positioning of organizations. Regardless of what the case might be, leaders must ensure that the focus of the adopted approaches is mainly on responding to requests in a timely manner, serving as a better platform for baseline service, and maintaining its operational efficiency. In other words, it focuses on cost reductions that enhance a better value for money, and it focuses on efficiency that aims at customer support excellence. Adopted approaches need to focus on personal developments and growing market opportunity.

STEP FOUR: SPECIFYING MEASURES

It's paramount for organizational leaders to identify and use appropriate measures for assessing the level at which organizations have achieved the desired objectives within a certain time frame. Achievement remains the major issue at any point because that's the need for productivity. Measures need to be reasonable and achievable and focus on the intended results. Measures need to reflect the capability and strength of strategic plans, objectives, and actions in terms of desired goals. However, measures need to be seen as a platform that will gauge organizational success. In a nutshell, measures are all performance effectiveness and could be measured in terms of sales volume, market share, cash flow, profit, ROI, dividends, and market value. Inappropriate measures will often lead managers to respond to situations incorrectly and will continue to reinforce undesirable behavior. Better measures could be driven by adopting an accurate system that would facilitate a perfect situation for designing, developing, and implementing new performance measurement system. It's also driven by the desire to meet customers' and other relevant stakeholders' needs and expectations whilst increasing productivity and positioning the organization better.

Adopted measures should enable leaders to precisely communicate performance expectations to various stakeholders to let various members know and understand what is expected from them at various situations in time. Communicating performance will enable leaders to identify performance gaps and also enable an organization to know and understand when and how to make decisions, in terms of where supports are required at a particular point in time.

STEP FIVE: EVALUATION

This is the process of collecting information from different sources within an organization to provide evidence of how various units have been able to perform to expectation. This information is then evaluated to identify where support is required. Evaluation processes need to be convenient for users in terms of their application, their need to be efficient by having the capacity of being responsible for managing the resources in terms of accountability, and their need to possess the ability to evolve by creating the space for effective development, testing, and introduction of new systems and future adjustments, that is, upgrades. This might occur over time for a number of reasons, such as a change in fashion, a change in the tastes of customers, and competitors' new developments and technologies.

Evaluation, being conducted on a regular basis, is a platform for improving the management and effectiveness of an organization and its operations. To do so, leaders are required to understand the differences between monitoring and evaluation. There is a huge need to make evaluation an integral part of an organization's functions, much as with planning and implementation and collecting of information required at different levels of an organization.

Strategy evaluation is as significant as strategy formulation because it throws light on the efficiency and effectiveness of the comprehensive plans in achieving the desired results. Leaders can also assess the appropriateness of current organizational strategies, which is a basic necessity in today's dynamic, socio-economic, innovative, and fast-changing world. According to various authors in the field of strategic management, evaluation is the final phase of strategic management; as such, it should be taken seriously.

STEP SIX: MAKING CHANGES

Continuous improvement needs to be an ongoing process that always requires continuous re-evaluation of goals and objectives so as to remain in a better position within any industry. Making success a goal in and of itself will not reflect the best of employees' abilities, but creating a reason for making adjustments after evaluation exercises will. Leaders need to careful about applying previous approaches in new challenges, because the need for change can arise anytime—new wine in an old bottle. Changes could be made easily once an effective consistency plan and the required resources are in place. Making changes within an organization requires hiring an external consultant to give accurate and updated advice in making the change process a reality at both formulation and implementation. Communication is always an important parameter; it allows team members and other stakeholders to understand the new policies and procedures that makeup the change process as a whole. Leaders need to go the extra mile in aligning the interests of stakeholders with the change process to avoid a breakdown in operational activities and also communicate in simple terms the benefits of compliance to the new system to all stakeholders. They need to know and understand the typical reasons for resistance to change, which are usually:

MISUNDERSTANDING THE NEED FOR CHANGE: Leaders can handle situations that are misunderstood by stakeholders by preparing to listen to the major concerns of various groups, be flexible in their views, and avoid contradicting themselves at any point in communicating the change process that is necessary for improvement. As it is commonly said, not taking steps is the most creative destruction because it allows situations within an organization to remain stagnant and ends up in failure in terms of achievements.

However, making use of one's own past experiences, culture, and personality often has a positive impact on how to make others listen to us because it's a better way of expanding one's view on the world at large. It's also a way to bridge the differences between leaders and stakeholders. Understanding the fear of others enables leaders to respond to members more effectively and solve the real problems that are presented, rather than staying stuck in disagreement and misunderstanding, which might end up resulting in confusion.

FEAR OF THE UNKNOWN: This always occurs when both leaders and team members lose focus and insight about the positive and transformational impact associated with their goals. In some cases it is a result of lack of knowledge about the responsibilities and requirements of leadership. In other words, a leader still holds onto leadership as a position rather than as a function to face down challenges facing an organization to and to deliver excellence in terms of execution. The fear of the unknown could be dealt with by leaders by uncovering the major cause of their fears; it is best to tackle their fears and later confront them with the best applicable technique or strategy. In addition to that, it is reasonable for leaders to surround themselves with like-minded people because they have the required insight and experience to understand the situation, which makes it easier to understand the emotional state regarding the situation. They are the best people to support and encourage one to remain focused, committed, and consistent in pursuing one's vision. They inspire by speaking possibilities and motivational words that make one develop an *'I can'* attitude, which increases one's strength to push through the tough spots to bypass any form of fear.

LACK OF COMPETENCE: This is a fear that is difficult for members to admit openly. But sometimes, change in organizations necessitates changes in skills, and some members might feel that their service might no longer be required by the organization. Therefore, the only way for affected members to try and survive is to react against the change. In this situation, leaders have a huge role to play developing themselves and others.

Incompetence is the inability of a leader to demonstrate persistently what is expected to transform an organization to its desired state. It's also the inability to identify the needs of various stakeholders at the right time and in the right measure. Such an approach will result in administrative chaos due to inappropriate planning. Incompetence can turn out to be a serious issue if continuous errors are not being dealt with at the appropriate time; dealing with it would put an end to poor judgment, the inability to work as part of a team, lack of skill or knowledge, and difficulty in communicating with others within an organization. Leaders need to identify a training need and set up a supervised support programme to reduce the level of incompetence and motivate members to be and remain committed to an organization's vision; the leader needs to do likewise.

POOR COMMUNICATION: This is a state whereby leaders find it difficult to value and communicate with their members. It involves ignoring emails and telephone messages from members and being unable to make effective contributions and suggestions at meetings. Poor communication does have a huge negative impact on an organization because stakeholders, especially employees, find it difficult to trust the leaders in office. Poor communication facilitates a state whereby members' intellectual efforts or opinions are not being seen as a relevant asset to the organization. This situation can also lead to a high rate of turnover due to the gap in communication. Poor communication can be handled by embracing the right coaching or training to improve the communication skills of any organizational member. In improving communication within an organization, leaders should strive to discover which communication method works best, encourage its usage, and ensure it produces results. Yet, the leader still needs to exercise understanding and patience by giving appropriate time for the method to work at its peak. Once a positive result is being recorded, leaders should remain consistent and persistent in that technique's continuous usage.

BENEFITS AND REWARDS: This is often seen as treat by team members because changes in the benefits and rewards system might lead to them working more for less. However, leaders need to ensure that due process is being followed, and the change process should never have an adverse effect on the future of members while with the organization: their stake needs to be respected. Having a better system would enable the organization to achieve effective performance from members alongside a high level of retention and also facilitate controllable expenses.

TAKE THIS HOME

No matter how productive a leader might be, he or she must make sure to take time and celebrate what others have helped them accomplish. It's important to reward team members so as to enable them to continue making their best effort.

In today's business environment, organizations need to undergo transformations to get, and stay, on top. The ability to achieve success for an organization mainly depends on a leader's ability to motivate others to see the light and reality in their vision, and enable others to have insight into what the big picture stands for regarding the future. However, motivation is the internal driving force or the aspiration towards making dreams and plans a reality. It is also the zeal to push action to occur. From experience, team members carrying out a specific task is never an issue; rather, leaving their home to go to the workplace has always been the issue. Therefore, leaders need to consider motivation an essential element for productivity.

To draw the cotton at this point, productivity is about being realistic in one's action, while avoiding assumptions. It about doing the right thing at the right time, sowing at the right season would enable harvest at the right time for a premium. But sowing while others are reaping reflects a lack of value of one's personality and ability. Either effectiveness or not, the ends justifies the means. Productivity is a measure that describes how well the resources of an organization are being used, or how well the available input performs to produce a specific output. Productivity can also be measured in quantitative terms, which qualifies it as a variable. Therefore, it can be defined and measured in absolute or relative terms. However, there is no universal definition of what productivity is, but it is all about achieving more with less, within a timeframe.

www.ingramcontent.com/pod-product-compliance
Lightning Source LLC
Chambersburg PA
CBHW061611220326
41598CB00024BC/3541